Introducing Famous Americans

Meet John Sutter

California Gold Rush Pioneer

Jane Katirgis and Chris Hayhurst

Enslow Publishing
101 W. 23rd Street
Suite 240
New York, NY 10011
USA
enslow.com

Published in 2020 by Enslow Publishing, LLC
101 W. 23rd Street, Suite 240, New York, NY 10011

Library of Congress Cataloging-in-Publication Data

Names: Katirgis, Jane, author. | Hayhurst, Chris, author.
Title: Meet John Sutter : California Gold Rush pioneer / Jane Katirgis and Chris Hayhurst.
Description: New York : Enslow Publishing, 2020 | Series: Introducing famous Americans | Includes bibliographical references and index. | Audience: Grades 3–5.
Identifiers: LCCN 2018060045| ISBN 9781978511446 (library bound) | ISBN 9781978511422 (pbk.) | ISBN 9781978511439 (6 pack)
Subjects: LCSH: Sutter, John Augustus, 1803–1880—Juvenile literature. | California—History—1846–1850—Juvenile literature. | Pioneers—California—Biography—Juvenile literature. | Swiss Americans—California—Biography—Juvenile literature. | California—Gold discoveries—Juvenile literature. | Sutter's Fort (Sacramento, Calif.)—Juvenile literature.
Classification: LCC F865.S93 K38 2020 | DDC 979.4/03092 [B] —dc23
LC record available at https://lccn.loc.gov/2018060045

Printed in the United States of America

To Our Readers: We have done our best to make sure all website addresses in this book were active and appropriate when we went to press. However, the author and the publisher have no control over and assume no liability for the material available on those websites or on any websites they may link to. Any comments or suggestions can be sent by email to customerservice@enslow.com.

Portions of this book originally appeared in *John Sutter: California Pioneer.*

Photo Credits: Cover, p. 1 (Sutter), p. 25 The Picture Art Collection/Alamy Stock Photo; cover, p. 1 (Sutter's Fort), p. 17 Library of Congress Prints and Photographs Division; p. 4 Artokoloro Quint Lox Limited/Alamy Stock Photo; p. 5 Hulton Deutsch/Corbis Historical/Getty Images; p. 6 ullstein bild Dtl/Getty Images; p. 7 Science & Society Picture Library/Getty Images; p. 8 Hulton Archive/Getty Images; p. 9 DEA/G. Dagli Orti/De Agostini/Getty Images; p. 11 Collection of the New-York Historical Society, USA/Bridgeman Images; p. 12 North Wind Picture Archives/Alamy Stock Photo; p. 13 Library of Congress/Corbis Historical/Getty Images; p. 15 Library of Congress Geography and Map Division; p. 18 Print Collector/Hulton Archive/Getty Images; pp. 19, 23 Bettmann/Getty Images; p. 20 MPI/Archive Photos/Getty Images; p. 22 Private Collection/Peter Newark American Pictures/Bridgeman Images; p. 24 VGhistory/Wikimedia Commons/File:Sutters hock farm1.jpg/CC BY-SA 3.0; p. 26 Bohemianroots/Wikimedia Commons/File:General_sutter_grave.jpg (detail)/CC BY-SA 3.0; p. 27 Pictures Now/Alamy Stock Photo; interior pages background pattern and graphic elements Ambient Ideas/Shutterstock.com.

Contents

1 John Sutter's Early Life

John Augustus Sutter was born on February 15, 1803, in a part of Germany called Baden. Most of John's family was from Switzerland. In 1818, John's parents sent him to Switzerland to go to school. When he was finished, he moved to the Swiss city of Basel. One day he met a woman named Anna Dübeld and fell in love.

This map of Europe shows Germany and Switzerland. Like Sutter, many Europeans immigrated to America in search of a better life.

After the Napoleonic Wars, Switzerland seemed peaceful and prosperous. This view of Basel, Switzerland, shows the Rhine River.

John and Anna were married in 1826. They immediately began raising a family. To make money, John worked as a printer. Unfortunately, he did not do well. Soon John owed people lots of money.

This portrait shows John Sutter in his Swiss army uniform before immigrating to the United States.

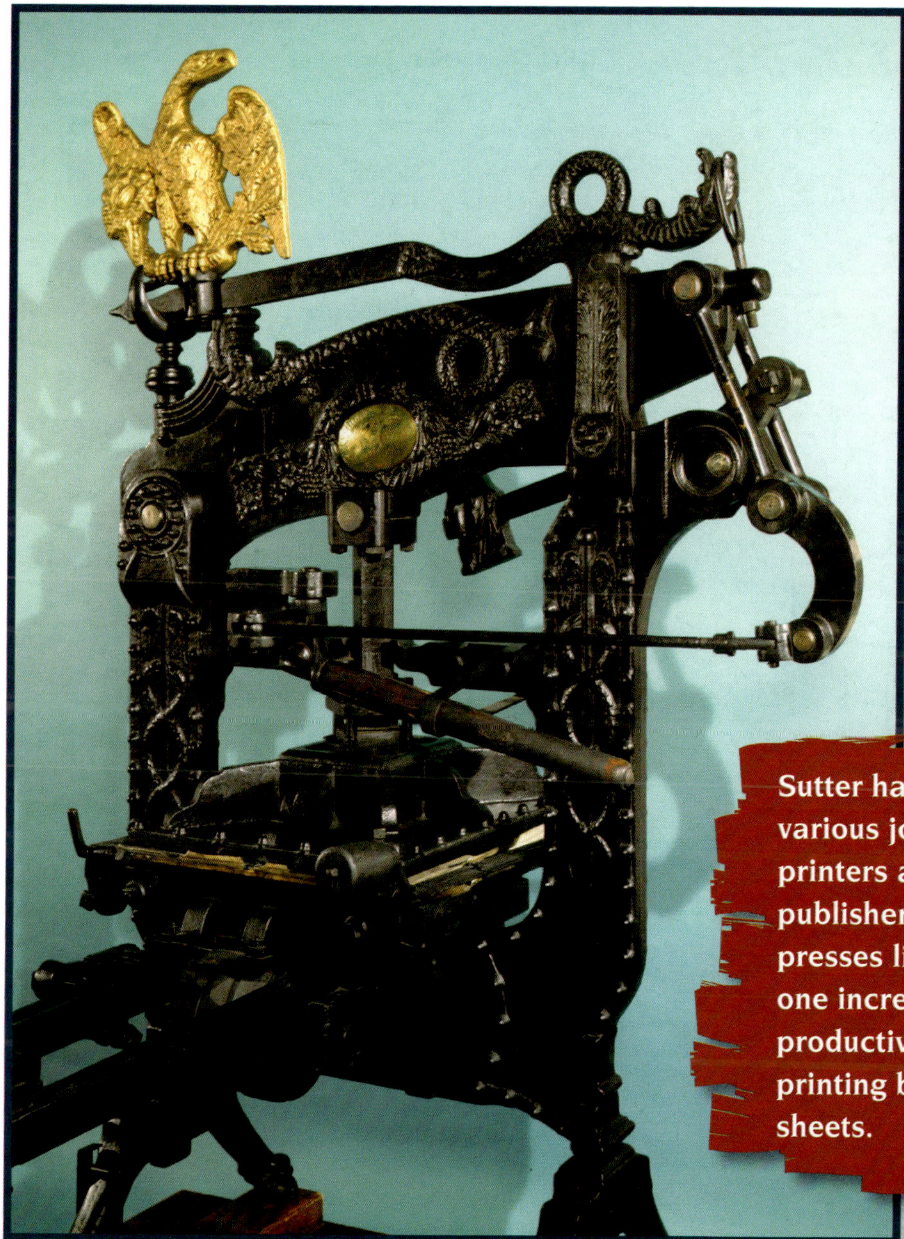

Sutter had various jobs with printers and publishers. Iron presses like this one increased productivity by printing bigger sheets.

In 1828, Sutter volunteered for the Swiss army. By 1834, Sutter owed so much money he feared he would be arrested. To escape the police, he left Anna and the children and sailed for the United States. He hoped he would find wealth in the New World.

A newspaper illustration depicts an immigrant ship crossing the Atlantic. Immigrants are crowded into the forward main deck.

Sutter joined the Swiss army to escape his creditors. Soon emigration seemed more attractive than army life. This illustration shows soldiers in the Swiss army in the early nineteenth century.

2 Going West

John Sutter sailed across the Atlantic Ocean. His ship arrived in New York in July 1834. Then he started to travel west. Sutter told people he was an officer in the Swiss army. "Call me Captain John Sutter," he said, even though he was not a captain. His first stop was in Missouri. He was low on cash, so he sold some of his possessions. He took the money he made to buy goods he could trade.

Let's Learn More

Most immigrants did not come to America to live in the cities, but to go west, obtain their own land, and farm for a living. Sutter received a huge grant of land (50,000 acres) from the Mexican government for his settlement.

Ships in New York Harbor are shown near Brooklyn Heights. In the sailing age, an immigrant's journey was long and dangerous.

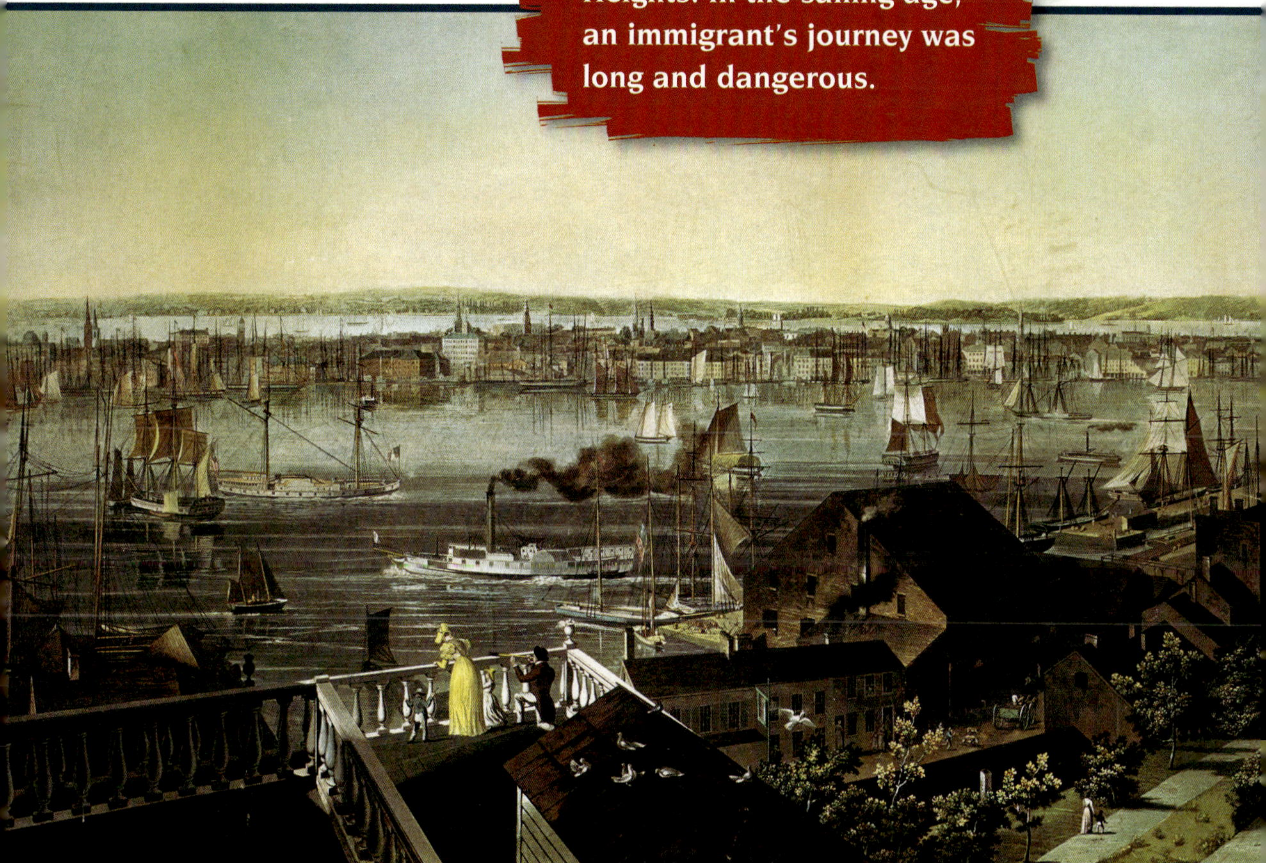

"Captain Sutter" was a natural at the trading business. He traveled from Missouri to the Mexican town of Santa Fe. There he traded goods for valuables like mules. Back in Missouri, the animals were worth lots of money.

The Santa Fe Trail is marked on this map. The trail was one of several major routes west for settlers, immigrants, and merchants.

Missouri traders rolled along the Santa Fe Trail in Conestoga wagons. John Sutter was such a trader for a number of years.

Sutter's wealth grew. But some people accused him of cheating and stealing. Sutter promised he would pay everyone back. But he never did. One day in 1838, he decided to leave town for good. He packed his bags and headed for California. California was then part of Mexico. Sutter would start a colony of settlers and become rich.

Let's Learn More

In the 1800s, settlers were required to live in Mexico for one year before they could become Mexican citizens. On August 29, 1840, almost exactly a year after his arrival in California, Sutter received his papers and became a Mexican citizen.

The western coast of America is shown on this map. The inset shows the Sacramento River, where Sutter built his farm.

3 New Helvetia

Five years after docking in New York, John Sutter arrived in Monterey. Monterey was the capital of California. Monterey's governor gave him permission to build his settlement. He showed Sutter a map. He pointed to a spot along the Sacramento River. There were Native Americans there, but there were also nearly 50,000 acres of land.

Let's Learn More

When Sutter came west on the Santa Fe Trail in the 1830s, many Native American tribes were hostile to the settlers, and it was a dangerous journey. Fighting between Native Americans and settlers continued until well after the Civil War.

Let's Learn More

Sutter's New Helvetia was named in honor of his European roots. The name means "New Switzerland."

Sutter had enough land to encourage other farmers to join him in California. This is Sutter's Fort.

Sutter named the area New Helvetia. Using Native Americans and other laborers, he built Sutter's Fort. Soon his colony had farms and thousands of cattle, horses, and sheep. Sutter called for more settlers to join the colony. He promised those who would stay that they could have work and free land.

This image of Sutter's Fort in 1847 shows the American flag flying over the fort.

In 1846, war broke out between the United States and Mexico. Near the war's end, the United States took control of California. It would be easier for Americans to move west. Sutter invited settlers to come to New Helvetia. But then something happened that would change his life forever.

Mexican general Antonio Lopez de Santa Anna led Mexican forces against the American invasion of his country in 1846.

American troops storm the Heights of Monterey in 1846, during the Mexican-American War. Americans won the war and added California and New Mexico to the United States.

4 The Gold Rush Is On

John Sutter had a carpenter who worked for him. The carpenter saw what looked to be gold on the ground. He took the gold to Sutter. Sutter told the worker to keep the discovery a secret. The secret got out. Soon word of the gold spread to San Francisco. The Gold Rush was on. People from all over rushed to California.

Let's Learn More

The man who found gold on Sutter's land was named James Marshall. Sutter had hired him to build a sawmill along the American River. A sawmill is a mill for cutting logs into boards.

Men pan for gold in California. Heavy gold particles would collect on the bottom of a pan when the dirt and other materials were washed away.

New Helvetia was overrun by thousands of people. Sutter's workers left him to look for gold. His colony was nearly destroyed in the frenzy. In 1849, Sutter abandoned his fort and moved to a farm.

AN ACCOUNT OF
CALIFORNIA,
AND THE
WONDERFUL GOLD REGIONS.

A New Arrival at the Gold Diggings.

WITH A DESCRIPTION OF
The Different Routes to California;
Information about the Country, and the Ancient and Modern Discoveries of Gold;
How to Test Precious Metals; Accounts of Gold Hunters;
TOGETHER WITH MUCH OTHER
Useful Reading for those going to California, or having Friends there.
ILLUSTRATED WITH MAPS AND ENGRAVINGS.
BOSTON:
PUBLISHED BY J. B. HALL, 66 CORNHILL.
For Sale at Skinner's Publication Rooms, 60½ Cornhill.
Price, 12½ cents.

The title page from an 1849 manual on gold mining is a reminder that gold encouraged many people to come west and settle in California.

Let's Learn More

John and Anna Sutter had four children. Their names were Johann Augustus Jr., Anna Eliza, Emil Viktor, and Wilhelm Alphonse.

Workers restore the farm Sutter moved to after he abandoned New Helvetia. He did not profit from the Gold Rush.

Finally, in 1850, Sutter's family came to the United States. They thought he would be living in luxury. Instead, he was a failed businessman. Captain Sutter was financially ruined.

This portrait of John Sutter was done in 1866, after bankruptcy and retirement. Sutter had a difficult life, having settled in the wrong place at the wrong time.

Sutter spent the rest of his life trying to repay his debts. In 1865, the Sutters' house burned down. John and Anna decided to leave California. They moved to Washington, DC, and then to Lititz, Pennsylvania. On June 18, 1880, John died. Anna died six months later. Today their graves can be found in a small cemetery in Lititz.

John Sutter and his wife are burried in Lititz, Pennsylvania. When they arrived in America, his wife and children found him penniless.

A modern reconstruction of Sutter's Fort stands near Sacramento. The Gold Rush made California one of the most populous states.

Timeline

1803—John Sutter is born.

1818—Sutter starts school in Switzerland.

1826—Sutter marries Anna Dübeld.

1828—Sutter volunteers for service in the Swiss army.

1834—Sutter arrives in the United States and travels west.

1839—Sutter arrives in Monterey, California, and starts his settlement.

1846—The Mexican-American War begins.

1849—Sutter leaves New Helvetia.

1865—The Sutters move to Washington, DC.

1880—Sutter dies at the age of 77.

Glossary

abandon (uh-BAN-dun) To leave without planning to come back.

colony (KAH-luh-nee) A group of people living in a new place.

Europe (YOOR-uhp) One of the seven continents.

financial (fy-NAN-shuhl) Having to do with money.

frenzy (FREHN-zee) Wild activity.

officer (AW-fih-sur) A person in charge of lower-ranking troops.

possessions (puh-ZEH-shunz) Things that a person owns.

settlement (SEH-tul-ment) A place occupied by settlers.

volunteer (vah-lun-TEER) To work for free or to agree to perform a task.

Learn More

Books

Blashfield, Jean F. *The California Gold Rush*. North Mankato, MN: Capstone Press, 2018.

Josh, Gregory. *If You Were a Kid During the California Gold Rush*. New York, NY: Children's Press, 2018.

Stoltman, Joan. *20 Fun Facts About the Gold Rush*. New York, NY: Gareth Stevens, 2018.

Websites

The California Gold Rush
pbs.org/wgbh/americanexperience/features/goldrush-california/
Read about this historic time in American history.

The Gold Rush
americanhistoryforkids.com/the-gold-rush/
Fun facts about the Gold Rush.

John Sutter: American Pioneer
britannica.com/biography/John-Sutter
Read about John Sutter and click on more links related to his life.

Primary Source Image List

Page 4: Engraving for *Mitchell's School and Family Geography*. Map dated 1840.

Page 8: *Emigrant Needlewomen on Deck*, from the *London Illustrated News*, 1850.

Page 9: *Carabinieri Voltigeurs*, 1840.

Page 11: *View of Manhattan from Brooklyn*, lithograph, 1837. Based on a watercolor by John William Hill, c. 1836.

Page 13: *March of the Caravan*, engraving from *Commerce of the Prairies*, by Josiah Gregg, c. 1844.

Page 15: A *New Map of Texas, Oregon and California*, published by S. Augustus Mitchell in 1846.

Page 17: Sutter's Fort, unknown photographer, 1867.

Page 19: Antonio Lopez de Santa Anna, based on the c. 1858 portrait by Paul L'Ouvrier.

Page 20: Based on the 1846 lithograph, *Storming of the Heights at Monterey*, by Nathaniel Currier.

Page 22: Panning for gold in California, 1849 photograph.

Page 23: Title page of *An Account of California and the Wonderful Gold Regions*, published by J.B. Hall in 1849.

Page 25: Portrait of John Augustus Sutter, by Frank Buscher,1866.

Index